A Cotman-Color Book with

text by **A. N. Court**

Oxford
in Colour

Jarrold Colour Publications, Norwich

St. Martin's Tower at Carfax, where four roads converge.
La tour St. Martin à Carfax, au croisement de quatre routes.
Turm von St. Martin in Carfax, wo vier Straßen zusammentreffen.

To walk through Oxford is to walk through history. Scarcely anywhere else in England is so much history, so much tradition and such a wealth of fine architecture to be found in a comparatively small area. Modern Oxford is a paradox, contriving to be two vastly different places at once; it is on the one hand a thriving industrial town, with its economy especially concerned with the manufacture of motor vehicles and its vision fixed on the future; at the same time it is one of the two leading university cities of the British Commonwealth, with its roots firmly fixed in the past.

The greatest problem facing twentieth-century Oxford, however, is not the maintenance of her architectural treasures; it is how to solve the problem of accommodation for the thousands of citizens and students, a task which is difficult enough; and how to cope with the ever-increasing volume of traffic which streams through the main highways of the city and throngs the narrow thoroughfares which link them. Every proposal to alleviate this situation seems to imperil some well-loved part of the city, and the problem can never be completely solved.

The early importance of Oxford depended on its name – a ford where oxen, and therefore men, could cross the Rivers Isis and Cherwell on their western and eastern flanks. In the troubled years before the Norman Conquest Oxford played an important part in the battles between the rival kingdoms of Mercia and Wessex, and later in the struggles against the Danes.

The University of Oxford had its beginnings in a number of religious communities which had been set up before the coming of the Normans. One of the earliest of these was the Convent of St. Frideswide which was in existence in the eighth century. The University's first charter was granted by the Pope in 1214, and about 1250 the Chancellor became independent of the Bishop of Lincoln. The thirteenth and fourteenth centuries were marked by frequent quarrels between the students and the townsfolk and even between rival student factions. One such incident in 1333 led to a number of students withdrawing to Stamford, which for a time threatened to rival Oxford as the premier seat of learning. Just over twenty years later occurred the riots on St. Scholastica's Day, when Town and Gown waged a murderous battle. The result to the town was humiliation, for the king gave his support to the Church and the University acquired considerable power over the town and its trade. Happily today these troubles are no more, and the people of Oxford speak proudly of 'their' University and are among the most zealous defenders of its privileged position. Nor do they stand alone, for the crumbling fabric of many of Oxford's historic colleges has been the reason for a world-wide appeal which has gained the support of people in every walk of life and of very many countries and races.

It is impossible to be dogmatic about the order of foundation of the various colleges, for several were formed from existing monastic halls and a few were re-foundations of former communities. Indeed the distinction of being the oldest foundation is disputed by Balliol, University, and Merton. Some account of the principal colleges of the University will be found in the pages which follow, but space does not permit the inclusion of every one, and some brief notes are appended of those which have had to be omitted.

Exeter College is named after the bishop of that city who founded it for poor students in 1314, and originally its Fellows were all West Country men. Climbing plants soften the somewhat plain appearance of many of its buildings, notable among which is the Chapel, the work of Sir George Gilbert Scott, who based his design on that of the Sainte Chapelle in Paris. The result is a building of noble proportions, enriched by fine stained-glass windows. There are three quadrangles at Lincoln College, the oldest of which was constructed at the time of its foundation in the fifteenth century by Richard Fleming, Bishop of Lincoln. The Hall still has its original fifteenth-century timber roof, although the interior was restored at the beginning of the eighteenth century.

It was the intention of Richard Fox, the founder of Corpus Christi in 1516, that the college should receive monks from Winchester, but he was persuaded by advice and money to admit secular clergy instead. A strong tradition of classical scholarship developed at Corpus and found practical expression in the appointment of a Lecturer in Greek who served the whole University. The Front Quadrangle with its embattled Gatehouse is unpaved, and in the centre stands an impressive sundial originally erected here in 1581 but restored in the following century. It incorporates a perpetual calendar and is surmounted by a pelican on a globe. Corpus Christi Chapel was considerably altered in the seventeenth century. Its treasures include a fine eagle-lectern, and altar-piece 'The Adoration of the Shepherds', attributed to Rubens, and the silver-gilt crozier which belonged to the founder. The Hall has a fine perpendicular hammerbeam roof and contains a good portrait of Richard Fox. The College Library, which is not open to the public, is not only a most attractive room, but it houses a valuable collection of early books, including some of the finest printed Classics and

Bibles, many of them autographed with famous names. Lord Nuffield, the founder of the college which bears his name is also remembered for his generosity to St. Peter's Hall, an Anglican foundation dating from 1929. It was built as a memorial to Bishop Chavasse of Liverpool, who had previously been rector of St. Peter-le-Bailey which now serves as the college Chapel. St. Peter's Hall became St. Peter's College in 1961.

Women students were not admitted into the University until the last quarter of the nineteenth century, when Lady Margaret Hall and Somerville were built. They were followed by St. Hugh's and St. Hilda's and they were all formally incorporated by Royal Charter in 1926. The modern Chapel of Lady Margaret Hall is Byzantine in its conception and has a triptych of the Nativity by Burne-Jones. All women's colleges were made full colleges of the University in 1960.

In the nineteenth century several Halls were founded as training centres for various denominations; these have now been granted the status of permanent Private Halls in the University, and one of them, Mansfield, although originally a Congregationalist college, has, since 1955, admitted students of secular subjects. There are also a number of newer colleges which cater principally for post-graduate studies and have students of both sexes. Linacre, St. Cross, St. Anthony's and Wolfson come into this category. Ruskin College was founded at the turn of the century by two Americans who greatly admired the work of John Ruskin, the philosopher and sociologist. It provides facilities to enable working men to study at Oxford.

At Oxford, as at Cambridge, the colleges are self-governing institutions, providing their Fellows and Dons with facilities for research, and preparing their undergraduates for their final examinations leading to a first degree. The governing body of the University as such consists of those graduates who have become Masters of Arts, and is known as Convocation. An inner council, the Hebdomadal Council, is the guiding hand in legislative matters. The titular head of the University is the Chancellor, who is elected by Convocation and is usually a prominent public figure. The Chancellor, however, presides only on formal occasions and it is the Vice-Chancellor who is the actual administrative Head of the University.

Academic life in Oxford is full and varied. Some of the occasions are solemn, some exciting and a few unashamedly frivolous. The three principal annual events are Commemoration, Congregation, and Convocation. The first is mainly concerned with the conferring of honorary degrees, the ceremony commemorating the opening of the Sheldonian Theatre in 1669.

Associated with it are the celebrations of the Encænia. Meetings of Congregation and Convocation are conducted with all the splendour and ceremony which tradition demands. The Oxford Union founded in 1823 as a social and debating club, has numbered among its presidents many who have subsequently become notable public figures.

The University Library is housed partly in the Old and New Bodleian and partly in the Radcliffe Camera which was completed in 1748. The funds for its erection and for the salary of a librarian were bequeathed by Dr. John Radcliffe, personal physician to Queen Anne. Radcliffe studied at University College, to which he also left considerable sums of money; he became a Fellow of Lincoln College and acquired a reputation for wit and original behaviour. The Radcliffe Camera is a striking building in the Palladian style and occupies an important position between St. Mary's Church and the Bodleian Library, to which it is linked by an underground passage. The Library of Oxford University shares with the libraries of Cambridge, Trinity College Dublin, the National Libraries of Scotland and Wales, and the British Museum the privilege of receiving a copy of every book published in the United Kingdom.

In the Middle Ages there was an increasing need in the University for 'schools' or lecture rooms, and in 1426 the University began the erection of the Divinity School which, however, was not opened until 1490. It is perhaps the most splendid single room in Oxford, and it has a magnificent stone roof. In this room Bishops Ridley, Latimer and Cranmer were interrogated, and here in 1681 the House of Commons met. Adjoining the Divinity School is Convocation House where degrees are conferred.

In the early seventeenth century Elias Ashmole bequeathed to the University the collection he had inherited. The Old Ashmolean Museum was built to house them, but some of the exhibits were later transferred to other museums, and the present-day Ashmolean is devoted to art and archaeology. The University Museum of Natural Science and the Pitt-Rivers Museum are in Parks Road.

Among the interesting buildings of Oxford are a number of old inns, most of which were formerly owned by various colleges and licensed by the University. The Mitre, once famous for its vintage wines and its thirteenth-century cellar, now offers a choice of restaurants, while the Golden Cross has one of the best preserved courtyards in the country. Here, it is said, Ridley, Latimer and Cranmer were accommodated before they were burned at the stake.

Magdalen College, founded in the fifteenth century, boasts a fine tower and attractive gardens.
Magdalen College, fondé au XVe siècle, possède un clocher magnifique et est entouré de jardins.
Magdalen College wurde im 15. Jahrhundert gegründet. Sein Schmuckstück ist sein Glockenturm.

The founder of Magdalen College was William of Waynflete, who incorporated into his buildings parts of the Hospital of St. John which once occupied the same site. The Kitchen may well belong to this former foundation. The visitor arriving by road from London is greeted, as he crosses the bridge over the River Cherwell, by the magnificent sight of Magdalen Bell Tower, erected at the beginning of the sixteenth century, and traditionally, though somewhat conjecturally, designed by Wolsey who was a scholar of the college. The Cloisters surrounding the Great Quadrangle date from the end of the fifteenth century. In the eighteenth century the fine Classical New Buildings were constructed along one side of a quadrangle to the north of the Cloisters. Near by is the Deer Park, an unusual feature of a university city. Magdalen Gardens are most attractive, and the Water Walks on the banks of the Cherwell are a pleasant retreat. One of the Walks is named after the essayist Addison, a former Fellow.

Merton was the first of the Oxford colleges in which the students were resident, as opposed to living in lodgings in the city. The founder was Walter de Merton, Chancellor to Henry III, but his first premises were at Malden in Surrey. The transition to Oxford took place about 1284. The buildings of Merton have a distinct medieval appearance, and fortunately they have largely escaped the hand of the 'improver'. Merton's greatest glory is the fourteenth-century Chapel, known in its earliest days as 'St. John within the Walls'. Originally it was intended to be a cruciform building, but the nave was never built. The Choir is magnificent and contains some remarkable windows. Mob Quad, an architectural gem, is the oldest of all in Oxford, contrasting in the simplicity of its architecture with the quadrangles of many other colleges.

Tradition asserts that University College was founded by King Alfred, and there is some evidence for the claim. More certain is it that the college as we know it today came into being in the latter years of the thirteenth century. The majority of the present buildings are Gothic in style and remarkably symmetrical, although part was constructed in the seventeenth and the rest in the nineteenth century. The Gatehouse in the centre of the North Range incorporates a statue of James II, dressed as a Roman. In the Chapel is a window depicting the story of Jonah, and others portray events from the Old and New Testaments. Tudor panelling from a former house on the site now embellishes the Common Rooms. One of the most famous former undergraduates of University College was the poet Shelley. He did not, however, take his degree, for he was 'sent down' for publishing *The Necessity of Atheism*. His connection with the college is commemorated by a marble statue.

Over the gateway in the North Range of University College stands a statue of James II.
Au-dessus de la loge septentrionale de University College est une statue de Jacques II.
Eine Statue von Jakob II. schmückt das Tor der Nordreihe des University College.

The front quadrangle of Oriel College was rebuilt in 1642 in Gothic style.
La première cour d'Oriel College fut restaurée en 1642 dans un style gothique.
Der vordere Hof des Oriel College scheint dem 14. Jahrhundert anzugehören, ist aber von 1642.

Oriel College was founded by Adam de Brome, almoner to Edward II. He had sworn to endow a college to the Virgin if she would help him escape from defeat at Bannockburn, and the original name of the college was 'The House of the Blessed Mary the Virgin in Oxford', but it has for centuries borne the name of Oriel, from 'La Oriole', a tenement on the site which was taken over in 1328. The Front Quadrangle was rebuilt in 1642 but in a style reminiscent of two hundred years earlier. The entrance to the Hall is surmounted by statues of Edward II and either James I or Charles I, with the Virgin Mary in a niche above. The Hall possesses a beautiful oak roof and a number of fine portraits. St. Mary's Hall, now incorporated in the college, existed as a separate institution for five hundred years. It is known by the curious name of 'Skimmery'. Oriel owns two fine drinking cups, one of which is believed to have been given by Edward II, whose portrait, together with those of other notable persons connected with the college, adorns the walls of the Hall.

The Cathedral Church of Christ Church is also the Chapel of the largest college in Oxford.
La cathédrale de Christ Church est aussi la chapelle du plus grand collège d'Oxford.
Die Kathedrale von Christ Church ist zugleich auch die Kapelle des College.

The largest college in Oxford is Christ Church, more properly 'The House of Christ's Cathedral in Oxford', but familiarly known as 'The House'. Its founder was Cardinal Wolsey, whose ambition was to build a college which would have no equal in magnificence. To this end he acquired the Priory of St. Frideswide and the endowments of more than forty of other monastic foundations. King Henry VIII refounded the college in 1532 and styled it 'King Henry VIII's College', and fourteen years later transferred to the college the See of Oxford, so that the College Chapel is also the Cathedral of the City and the Dean of the Cathedral is also Head of 'The House'.

Naturally it is the Cathedral Church which is the pride of Christ Church. It is the smallest of the older English cathedrals and is an interesting example of an ecclesiastical building which is a harmony of several different styles. Traces of Saxon work are discernible in the Choir, while the Tower is unmistakably Norman, though crowned with an Early English spire. The most notable monument is the Shrine of St. Frideswide which formerly stood in the Lady Chapel. The shrine, which dates from the thirteenth century, has remarkable carvings of trees and plants.

Before the fourteenth century there was in Oxford a Hall called Segreve or Segrym which became Broadgates Hall and existed right through until 1624 when, in the reign of James I it was incorporated in Pembroke College. The college, founded by Thomas Tesdale, is named after the Earl of Pembroke who was Chancellor of the University at the time of its foundation. Like most of the college buildings the Chapel is of eighteenth-century date, but in 1884 the interior was altered and re-decorated and the fine windows, the work and gift of Kempe, a former scholar, were installed. The Master's Lodging is a house in St. Aldates; this was once Wolsey's Almhouse and was purchased from Christ Church in 1888. The most celebrated student of Pembroke was Dr. Samuel Johnson, who came to the college in 1728 but was forced, through lack of means, to leave at the end of the following year. Dr. Johnson's quarters were a small second-floor room over the gateway, and in the Library, which was once the refectory of Broadgates Hall, we can see the desk which he used and some of his original manuscripts. A portrait of him by Reynolds hangs in the Senior Common Room, where his famous teapot is also preserved.

Pembroke College was named after a university Chancellor of the seventeenth century.
Pembroke College, fondé par Tesdale of Woodstock, porte le nom du chancelier de l'époque.
Pembroke College wurde nach dem Grafen von Woodstock, dem damaligen Kanzler, benannt.

Founded by the late Lord Nuffield in 1937, Nuffield College was intended for post-graduate studies. The original plans were Byzantine in character, but were rejected by the founder and the college was finally built in a somewhat austere and functional manner.

Brasenose is a sixteenth-century foundation on the site of a number of medieval Halls. One of these is commemorated in the name, which, in spite of attempts to associate it with a brewery, probably means just 'brazen nose'. There is, indeed, a representation of a brass nose over the Gateway and another above the High Table in the Hall. There were two founders; Sir Richard Sutton and William Smythe, Bishop of Lincoln.

The official University Church of St. Mary was founded according to tradition by Alfred the Great.
Selon la tradition, l'église officielle de l'Université fut fondée par Alfred le Grand.
St. Mary's, die offizielle Universitätskirche, soll aus der Zeit Alfreds des Grossen stammen.

The official University Church is St. Mary the Virgin in 'The High'. Its fine 180-foot spire was built in the thirteenth century and is a prominent land mark from whatever spot it is viewed. Although St. Mary's is mentioned in the Domesday survey, the main parts of the church date from the latter half of the fifteenth century. On Sunday mornings in term time the University sermon is preached in St. Mary's and the opening of the University term is marked by a solemn service. Before the opening of The Sheldonian Theatre St. Mary's was not only the religious centre of University life but also its administrative centre. According to tradition the church was founded in the time of Alfred the Great, but the architecture is in the main of the fifteenth century. It has beautifully wrought twisted pillars and a statue of the Virgin and Child which figured in the charges against Archbishop Laud.

'The most beautiful street in the world'. Such has been the verdict of more than a few discerning visitors, and few can deny that the principal street of Oxford, affectionately known as 'The High' but more correctly as High Street, has dignity, beauty and interest of the first order. It runs from east to west, crossing the principal north-south thoroughfare at Carfax, meaning 'four roads'. At Carfax stands a tower, all that remains of the medieval church of St. Martin. To the north Cornmarket Street leads towards Balliol, Trinity and St. John's Colleges and to the Ashmolean Museum; St. Aldates leads southwards to Pembroke and Christ Church. The old 'Sheep Shop' in St. Aldates was without any doubt used by Tenniel for his illustrations of Lewis Carroll's *Alice in Wonderland*. Carroll (Charles Dodgson) was a student, and later a don, of Christ Church. 'The High' is undoubtedly one of the finest streets to be found in any English city, and the view from Magdalen Tower underlines the great variety of architecture which Oxford has to show. Rising high above the colleges are the spire of St. Mary's Church and the Classical dome of the Radcliffe Camera. To the north of and parallel with 'The High' lies Holywell Street with a number of fine old houses, notable among them the 'Old Music Room'.

The 180-foot-high spire of St. Mary's Church dominates the architecture of 'The High'.
La fléche de l'église de St. Mary, haute de 180 pieds, domine « The High ».
Der 180-Fuss hohe Spitzturm der Marienkirche ragt über den Gebäuden der „High" empor.

All Souls is unique as a college, in the modern sense of the term, for it has no undergraduates. In many ways it is akin to the medieval establishments which preceded the colleges and whose members were graduates or Fellows. Its founder was Archbishop Chichele, and its purpose twofold; firstly to commemorate the military victories of Henry V, and secondly as a chantry where masses were to be said for the souls of those who had fallen in the French Wars.

Queen's College was founded in 1340 by Robert de Eglesfield, Chaplain to Philippa the wife of Edward III. Nothing remains of the early building and the entire architecture of Queen's is in the Classical style of the late seventeenth and early eighteenth centuries. The fine frontage is attributed to Hawkesmoor, a pupil of Sir Christopher Wren who was responsible for the Chapel, the Library and the Hall.

At the beginning of the fourteenth century there were more than eighty medieval Halls in Oxford and most of these were subsequently incorporated in the larger colleges. One, however, survives in its original form. This is St. Edmund Hall situated in Queen's Lane just inside the line of the old city wall. St. Edmund Hall is named after St. Edmund of Abingdon, who was a tutor at Oxford before he became Archbishop of Canterbury and the college is believed to occupy the site of his residence. The Hall was the property of Osney Abbey, a twelfth-century Augustinian house of which only a few relics remain in the west of the town, but at the time of the Dissolution it was saved from extinction by Queen's College, which continued to appoint the Principal until 1938, when independence was granted and St. Edmund Hall became an autonomous college. The buildings range in date from the sixteenth to the twentieth centuries and nothing of the medieval Hall now remains. The Chapel, dating from the seventeenth century, contrasts pleasantly with the Tudor buildings which adjoin it on the northern side.

In the fourteenth century William of Wykeham rebuilt Winchester Cathedral and founded Winchester School and New College, Oxford. The association between the school and the college continues to this day, but New College, which once had the privilege of conducting its own examinations, now draws its undergraduates from many other places besides Winchester. The college chapel, though considerably restored, is still one of the finest in Oxford. The reredos, which fills the east wall, has over fifty figures of apostles, prophets, saints, kings and angels, with the enthroned Christ in the centre of the topmost row. When the interior of the Chapel was restored in the last century the medieval misericords were fortunately preserved. New College Hall is a splendid example of fourteenth-century building, but its oak roof is modern. Of particular interest is the linenfold panelling. The peaceful cloisters remain much as the founder left them, a place for quiet meditation.

Hertford is the modern successor to a foundation which came into being as long ago as 1284, when Hart Hall was founded by Elias de Hertford. In the eighteenth century Hart Hall became Hertford College, but at the beginning of the nineteenth century its premises were acquired by Magdalen Hall. In 1874 Magdalen Hall was dissolved and Hertford was refounded, largely through the munificence of a banker, Charles Baring. Though many of the buildings of Hertford College are understandably modern, the Elizabethan era is represented by the Library which was formerly Hart Hall. Linking the new buildings on the further side of New College Lane with the older ranges is the stone 'Venetian Bridge', reminiscent of the bridge at St. John's College, Cambridge, and of the famous 'Bridge of Sighs' at Venice.

The Sheldonian and the Classical Clarendon Building are two of Oxford's best-known landmarks.
Deux repères d'Oxford bien-connus sont le Théâtre Sheldonian et le Clarendon Building.
Zwei bekannte Wahrzeichen Oxfords sind das Sheldonian Theater und das Clarendon Building.

Broad Street leads from St. Giles Street to Parks Road and near its junction with the latter are two of Oxford's best known landmarks, the Sheldonian Theatre and the Clarendon Building. The former, a semicircular amphitheatre designed by Sir Christopher Wren, was the first building of its kind to be erected in the seventeenth century. It resembles in style the Temple of Marcellus at Rome. On the railings in front of the building are effigies of Roman emperors. Adjoining the Sheldonian is the Clarendon Building which dates from 1713. It was originally the home of the Clarendon Press, but now houses the Proctor's Office and the Registry of the University. The portico of this imposing eighteenth-century building is supported by four Doric columns and the roof is embellished with figures of the Muses. Opposite the Clarendon Building stands the New Bodleian, opened by His Majesty King George VI in 1946. It forms part of the University Library.

Only one Oxford college, Jesus, came into being in the reign of Queen Elizabeth I. Its first benefactor was Hugh Price, a Welshman, and the college has always had a close association with the Principality, numbering many well-known Welshmen among its former students, including T. E. Lawrence ('Lawrence of Arabia') and Richard 'Beau' Nash. Jesus Chapel and Hall both date from the early seventeenth century. In the nineteenth century the Chapel was enlarged and restored and the former west door was blocked up. It has some excellent carving, a panelled pulpit and memorials to former principals including one to Sir Eubule Thelwall who was responsible for building the Principal's Lodging near by. The Hall has largely remained in its original form and contains interesting portraits, including those of Elizabeth I, Charles I and Charles II, and has a fine carved screen on which can be seen the arms of Dr. Griffith Powell, who was Principal of the college at the time when the Hall was built. The college also owns a huge silver punch bowl, dating from the eighteenth century. The Library houses a fine collection of Welsh manuscripts.

The north façade of Worcester College Quadrangle reveals the Classical style.
La façade nord de Worcester College montre le style classique du XVIIIe siècle.
Die Nordfassade des Hofes von Worcester College zeigt den klassischen Stil.

Monastic Orders were responsible for the foundation of many of the colleges of Oxford, and Worcester is no exception, for it began its existence as a cell of Gloucester Abbey. In the fifteenth century this became Gloucester Hall which continued until the foundation of Worcester College in 1714. The main buildings are in the Classical style of the eighteenth century, but on one side of the quadrangle is a range of monastic camerae, known as the 'Cottages'. In medieval times each of these houses was assigned to a particular Benedictine community. The Chapel is extensively decorated with paintings and mosaics, the whole conception of the design representing Man and Nature praising God, and the Hall contains armorial bearings of Benedictine Abbeys and of former members of the College. Worcester shares with University College a quaint custom dating from the Middle Ages; every morning the undergraduates are awakened by the hammering of a wooden mallet on the door of each staircase. The college gardens are spacious and contain an attractive lake.

The earliest records of Balliol College show that it was founded about 1265 by John de Balliol as part of a penance he had to pay to the Bishop of Durham. The original foundation for poor scholars was remodelled on similar lines to Merton, the scholars being subject for the first time to regulations of discipline and conduct. These rules were the forerunners of the code of behaviour which is today accepted as normal in a residential university. Balliol's widow, Devorguilla, carried on the work he had begun and thus shares with her husband the honour of the foundation. Most of the buildings of Balliol date from the nineteenth century, and architecturally Balliol is a none-too-happy mixture of styles, but it possesses one of the best quadrangles in Oxford. Fortunately the medieval Old Hall still stands and now has become the Library. In front of the College stands the Martyrs' Memorial erected to the memory of Bishops Latimer and Ridley, and later Cranmer, nearly three hundred years after their martyrdom. The architect was Sir Giles Scott, and his graceful monument incorporates statues, by Weekes, of the three Bishops.

Balliol College was founded by John de Balliol in 1265 and completed by his wife, Devorguilla.
Balliol College fut fondé en 1265 par John de Balliol, puis achevé par sa veuve, Devorguilla.
Balliol College wurde 1265 von John de Balliol gegründet und später von seiner Witwe ausgebaut.

St. John's was originally St. Bernard's College, founded in 1437 on the site of a Benedictine house. In the sixteenth century it passed into the hands of Christ Church but was refounded in 1555 by Sir Thomas White, a wealthy member of the Merchant Taylors Company. St. John's is still closely linked with the Merchant Taylors' School. It was during the Presidency of William Laud, early in the seventeenth century, that the buildings of Canterbury Quadrangle were completed. The centre feature of the East Front incorporates a statue of Charles I, and in the range opposite is the figure of Henrietta Maria. Canterbury Quad is a magnificent example of the Italian style of architecture and is justly famous. The Garden Front of the East Range faces the college garden, the largest in Oxford. St. John's College Chapel is situated in the Front Quad, where the Gatehouse and the south and west sides date from the foundation of St. Bernard's College. The Chapel, which has been altered on several occasions, was refaced in Gothic style in the nineteenth century.

Trinity College came into being in the sixteenth century when Sir Thomas Pope, a rich local landowner, refounded it as a successor to Durham College. The latter, a thirteenth century monastic institution for Benedictines, had been suppressed at the Dissolution. A few of the buildings of the earlier foundation which were incorporated into the new college are still in existence; these include the Old Library on the east side of the small quadrangle. The eighteenth century architecture of Trinity College belies its seventeenth-century date. It is generally accepted that it was designed by Wren and it contains some of the finest carving by Grinling Gibbons. The West Tower of the Chapel is crowned with female statues representing Geometry, Astronomy, Theology and Medicine. The last is a modern reproduction of the original which is now in the President's Garden. Features of the college are the beautiful wrought-iron gateway which gives access to New Quad, and a charming group of seventeenth-century 'cottages', formerly students' halls, which have happily been preserved and incorporated into the college.

In the sixteenth century Trinity succeeded Durham College, and some old buildings remain.
Au XVIe siècle Trinity College succéda à Durham College et certains bâtiments subsistent.
Einige Gebäude des Trinity College stammen aus der Zeit seines Vorgängers.

Wadham is yet another college which occupies the site of a former religious establishment, but historically it has no official connection with its predecessor. It was Nicholas Wadham, a Somerset man who planned the college, but it was his widow, Dorothy, who carried out his plans and founded Wadham in 1610, and she employed Somerset craftsmen to create the tasteful architecture which delights us today.

Keble College was founded in the late nineteenth century to combine a university education with the principles of the Church of England. It was built by public subscription as a memorial to the Reverend John Keble, the author of *The Christian Year*, and became fully self-governing as recently as 1952. Its buildings are among the most striking in Oxford. The red brick is ornamented with patterns of black and white stones and the whole effect is quite unusual.

The University boathouses are situated on the Isis, between Folly Bridge and Iffley, for this river is primarily the province of the oarsman. Rowing is taken very seriously by many undergraduates and there is great rivalry between college crews. The principal contests take place during 'Eights Week' in May, when the annual Summer Eights are the excuse for wildly enthusiastic scenes on both banks of the river. Each boat endeavours to 'bump' the one immediately in front, and ultimately to achieve the distinction of becoming 'Head of the River'. The week ends with the traditional 'Bump Summer' when the leading crew celebrates its victory. The height of a rowing man's ambition is to gain his 'blue', that is to row against Cambridge in the annual contest on the Thames from Putney to Mortlake which takes place annually in the spring.